C O N T E N T S

PART I

PART II

photo credit: robert antonio photography

ABOUT THE AUTHOR

AILENE TORRES, THE AUTHOR OF THIS INFORMATIVE EBOOK, IS A
MULTI-TALENTED DYNAMO IN THE WORLDS OF MODELING,
JOURNALISM, AND EVENT PRODUCTION. WITH A CAREER THAT HAS
SPANNED THE GRITTY WORLD OF INVESTIGATIVE REPORTING,
GLAMOROUS RUNWAYS, AND INTERNATIONAL MODELING, AILENE
BRINGS A WEALTH OF EXPERIENCE AND KNOWLEDGE TO THE TABLE.

HER EXPERTISE IS NOT CONFINED TO THE WRITTEN WORD ALONE;
AILENE HAS MASTERFULLY ORCHESTRATED NUMEROUS CASTING
CALLS, INCLUDING DURING THE WORLD-RENOWNED MIAMI SWIM
WEEK. HER FASHION SHOWS HAVE GIVEN OPPORTUNITIES TO 100S OF
MODELS STARTING OUT AND SHE HAS WORKED WITH PROFESSIONAL
MODELS ESTABLISHED IN THEIR CAREERS. HER UNIQUE BLEND OF
INSIGHT INTO THE FASHION INDUSTRY AND HER GIFT FOR
NARRATIVES MAKE HER THE PERFECT INSIDER TO UNVEIL THE
SECRETS OF MODELING SUCCESS.

1

INTRODUCTION:
DISCOVER THE WORLD OF MODELING

Welcome to the thrilling world of modeling! Whether you're a man or a woman, embarking on a career in modeling can be an incredibly rewarding and exciting journey. This industry offers a platform for self-expression, creativity, and the opportunity to make your mark in the glamorous world of fashion and entertainment.

Modeling is a diverse field that encompasses a wide range of opportunities, from high-fashion runways and glossy magazine covers to niche markets and digital platforms. It's a world where beauty comes in all shapes, sizes, and forms, and where your uniqueness is not only celebrated but also highly sought after.

INTRODUCTION:
DISCOVER THE WORLD OF MODELING

This guide is designed to be your companion as you take your first steps into modeling, providing you with a comprehensive roadmap to navigate this dynamic industry. Whether you're dreaming of strutting down runways, gracing the pages of fashion magazines, or becoming the face of a major brand, you'll find valuable insights and practical advice here.

Throughout this journey, you'll learn how to create a professional comp card that showcases your versatility, perfect your poses, refine your runway walk, and decide whether you're better suited for print, runway, or niche modeling. We'll explore the nuances of preparing for castings, from choosing the right outfit to deciding whether to wear makeup and how to style your hair.

But modeling is more than just appearances. It's about confidence, professionalism, and resilience. You'll gain insights into maintaining your physical and mental well-being, building a standout portfolio, working with agencies, and navigating the fashion industry's ever-changing landscape.

This guide is for everyone, regardless of your background, age, or experience level. Whether you're a seasoned professional looking to up your game or a complete newcomer with a dream, we're here to help you take those bold steps toward a successful modeling career.

1

INTRODUCTION:
DISCOVER THE WORLD OF MODELING

So, are you ready to embark on this thrilling journey? Let's dive into the world of modeling and explore the opportunities that await you. Get ready to unleash your inner star and discover the limitless potential that modeling has to offer. Your adventure begins now!

- Tip: Start your modeling journey by understanding the industry's demands and expectations.

2

CREATING A PROFESSIONAL COMP CARD

In the modeling industry, your comp card is your calling card —a powerful tool that introduces you to potential clients, agencies, and casting directors. It's essential to create a comp card that not only captures your unique look but also leaves a lasting impression. In this chapter, we'll guide you through the process of crafting a compelling and professional comp card that opens doors to opportunities.

UNDERSTANDING THE COMP CARD
A comp card, short for composite card or zed card, is a multi-purpose marketing tool that typically consists of a single 8.5 x 5.5-inch card with several images showcasing your versatility. It provides essential information about you, including your name, contact details, vital statistics, and a selection of your best photographs.

CREATING A PROFESSIONAL COMP CARD

ELEMENTS OF A COMP CARD
1. Photos: The heart of your comp card is the collection of high-quality photos. These should demonstrate your range as a model, showcasing different looks, styles, and expressions. Aim for a mix of headshots, full-body shots, and various angles to display your versatility.

Tip: Invest in a professional photographer who specializes in modeling portfolios. Quality images can make a significant difference.

2. Name and Contact Information: Ensure your full name is prominently displayed on the card. Include your agency's name and contact information if applicable. Always provide a working phone number and a professional email address.
Tip: Keep your contact information updated. A potential client needs to reach you easily.

3. Vital Statistics: Include your height, weight, measurements (bust, waist, hips for women; chest, waist, inseam for men), and shoe size. Accurate measurements are crucial, as they help clients determine your suitability for specific assignments.

Tip: Update your measurements regularly and be honest about them. Remember, brands and designers are open to inclusive body shapes and sizes, so the truth can help you stand out!

4. Agency Logo (if applicable): If you're signed with an agency, their logo or branding should be included. It adds credibility and shows you're a professional model. For example, although, the Pur Fae Collective isn't a traditional agency, we provide members with a professional designed and branded composite card for our members' use.

DESIGNING YOUR COMP CARD
- Layout: Keep the layout clean and uncluttered. Choose a simple, elegant design that doesn't distract from your photos.
- Images: Select your best and most recent images. Ensure they accurately represent your current look and style.
- Font and Text: Use legible fonts for your name and contact information. Avoid fancy or hard-to-read fonts.
- Color Scheme: Stick to a color scheme that complements your images. Neutral tones often work best.

COMP CARD VARIATIONS
- Digital Comp Cards: In today's digital age, having a digital version of your comp card is essential. Create a PDF or an online portfolio with clickable links to your website or social media but make sure you have both versions. Do not solely rely on a digital comp card.
- Printed Comp Cards: Traditional printed comp cards are still valuable for in-person castings and meetings. Invest in high-quality printing for a professional finish. Do not do mass production because as you update images and

measurements, a heavy investment in a comp card printing could be a waste when the information on the card becomes outdated with your latest gig.

UPDATING YOUR COMP CARD
Regularly update your comp card to reflect changes in your appearance, style, or portfolio. This ensures your card remains an accurate representation of your current self. Your comp card is your first impression in the modeling world. It should reflect your professionalism, versatility, and commitment to your craft. Invest time, effort, and resources in creating a comp card that not only captures your essence but also leaves a lasting mark on anyone who sees it. With a well-designed comp card in hand, you're ready to make your mark in the industry.

3

POSE LIKE A PRO

Posing is an art form that can transform a good photograph into an extraordinary one. As a model, your ability to strike captivating poses is a fundamental skill that can set you apart in the competitive world of modeling. In this chapter, we'll explore the techniques and tips to help you pose like a professional model.

1. Understand Your Body
The first step in mastering posing is understanding your body. Every body is unique, and learning how to accentuate your strengths and minimize your perceived flaws is key. Spend time in front of a mirror, experimenting with different angles and movements to discover what works best for you.

2. Practice Regularly
Like any skill, practice makes perfect. Dedicate time to practice posing in various styles, from fashion to editorial to commercial. Practice in front of a mirror, enlist a friend to be your photographer, or hire a professional photographer for a portfolio-building session.

3. Learn the Basics
Professional models have a repertoire of classic poses they can draw from at any moment. These include:
- The S-Curve: Creating an S-shaped curve with your body by shifting your weight to one leg and tilting your hips.
- Hands and Arms: Knowing what to do with your hands and arms is crucial. Avoid letting them hang limply; instead, engage them to create dynamic lines.
- Facial Expressions: Practice various facial expressions, from serene to playful to intense. Your face can convey a range of emotions, adding depth to your poses. Practice with a camera so you can see how your facial expressions present when captured. Adjust accordingly.

4. Study Posing Guides
Study posing guides, books, and online tutorials to gain insights into professional posing techniques. Learning from the experts can provide valuable guidance and inspiration.

5. Work with a Mirror

A mirror is an excellent tool for self-assessment. Pose in front of a mirror to see how your body looks from different angles. Pay attention to your posture, facial expressions, and the lines your body creates.

6. Use Props and Environments

Incorporate props and the environment into your poses. These elements can add interest and context to your photos. For example, holding a bouquet of flowers or leaning against a wall can create visually appealing compositions.

7. Embrace Natural Movements

Avoid rigid poses. Instead, incorporate natural movements into your posing, such as walking, twirling, or running your fingers through your hair. These actions can add dynamism to your shots.

8. Focus on the Eyes

Your eyes are a powerful tool for conveying emotion. Practice making strong, confident eye contact with the camera. Experiment with different gazes, from direct to slightly off-camera.

9. Seek Feedback

Don't hesitate to seek feedback from photographers,

mentors, or peers. Constructive criticism can help you refine your posing techniques and identify areas for improvement.

10. Stay Relaxed and Confident
Posing can feel unnatural at first, but it's essential to stay relaxed and confident. Tension can be visible in photographs, so take deep breaths, shake out any stiffness, and exude confidence in your body language.

11. Practice Posing Transitions
When working with photographers, practice smooth transitions between poses. This helps maintain a fluid and efficient photoshoot, capturing a variety of shots quickly.

12. Be Open to Direction
During professional shoots, be receptive to the photographer's direction. They may have a specific vision or pose in mind that can lead to outstanding results.

Mastering the art of posing is an ongoing journey. It's a combination of understanding your body, practicing regularly, and continuously refining your techniques. With dedication and perseverance, you can pose like a professional model, elevating your modeling career to new heights. So, strike a pose, and let your unique personality and style shine through!

4

PERFECT YOUR RUNWAY WALK

The runway walk is the signature skill of a fashion model. It's your opportunity to captivate audiences, leave a lasting impression, and showcase the designer's creations. In this chapter, we'll explore the techniques and tips to help you perfect your runway walk, whether you're strutting the catwalk during fashion week or at a local fashion show.

Understanding Runway Walk Styles
Before diving into the mechanics of a runway walk, it's crucial to understand the various runway walk styles and their differences:

1. High Fashion Walk: High fashion runway walks are known for their dramatic and distinctive style. These walks often involve slow, deliberate steps, a straight posture, and exaggerated poses at the end of the runway.

2. Commercial Walk: Commercial runway walks are more natural and relatable. They typically require a friendlier, approachable demeanor with a moderate pace and a hint of personality.

3. Couture Walk: Couture runway walks are characterized by elegance and poise. They demand precise, graceful movements and often incorporate intricate choreography.

Steps to Perfect Your Runway Walk

1. Posture and Alignment:
 - Maintain Straight Posture: Keep your shoulders back, spine straight, and chin level. Good posture is the foundation of a strong runway walk.
 - Balanced Steps: Walk with your feet in a straight line, one foot in front of the other, creating a narrow runway-like path. Your steps should be evenly spaced.

2. Arm Placement:
 - Natural Swing: Let your arms swing naturally as you walk. Avoid stiff, exaggerated arm movements. Keep your hands relaxed and fingers gently extended.
 - Elbows In: Keep your elbows close to your body rather than letting them flare out. This creates a cleaner, more elegant look.

PERFECTING YOUR RUNWAY WALK

3. Head and Eye Contact:
 - Forward Gaze: Fix your gaze straight ahead, slightly above the audience's eye level. Maintain a confident and focused expression.
 - Avoid Looking Down: Resist the urge to look down at your feet. Trust your steps and maintain eye contact with the audience.

4. Stride Length:
 - Balanced Steps: Take measured, consistent strides. Avoid taking steps that are too long or too short, which can disrupt your rhythm.
 - Practice Walking in Heels: If you're walking in heels, practice extensively to ensure stability and confidence.

5. Hip Movement:
 - Subtle Hip Swing: Add a slight hip sway to your walk. This subtle movement adds grace and femininity to your stride.
 - Don't Overdo It: Avoid excessive hip movement, which can appear unnatural.

6. Pace and Timing:
 - Match the Music: If there's music accompanying your runway walk, aim to match your pace and movements to the beat. This synchronicity can enhance the overall presentation.

- Practice Timing: Rehearse your walk with a consistent sense of timing, so you're not rushing or moving too slowly.

7. Confidence and Attitude:
- Confidence is Critical: Exude confidence and self-assuredness throughout your walk. Your attitude and presence are just as important as your movements.
- Maintain Composure: Even if you stumble or face unexpected situations on the runway, maintain composure and continue walking confidently.

Perfecting your runway walk takes practice and patience. Rehearse your walk regularly, seek feedback from experienced models or instructors, and record yourself to identify areas for improvement. Attend modeling workshops and runway classes to refine your skills further.

Your runway walk is your calling card in the world of fashion modeling. It's an art form that requires dedication, precision, and individuality. By mastering the techniques and styles of runway walking, you can confidently step onto any catwalk, leaving an indelible mark with each stride. Remember, practice makes perfect, so embrace the journey of perfecting your runway walk as an integral part of your modeling career.

- *Tip: Practice, Practice, Practice*

5

MODELING NICHE: RUNWAY, PRINT, OR BEYOND

In the vast and diverse world of modeling, there are numerous niches to explore, each offering its unique opportunities and challenges. As you embark on your modeling journey, it's essential to identify the niche that aligns with your strengths, interests, and aspirations. In this chapter, we'll guide you through the process of choosing your modeling niche, whether it's runway, print, or something entirely distinctive.

UNDERSTANDING DIFFERENT MODELING NICHES

1. Runway Modeling:
 - The Catwalk: Runway models showcase clothing and accessories by walking down the runway during fashion shows. It's all about projecting confidence, elegance, and grace.

MODELING NICHE: RUNWAY, PRINT, OR BEYOND

- Physical Requirements: Runway models typically have specific height and measurement requirements. It's essential to meet these standards to excel in this niche.
- Opportunities: Runway modeling offers exposure to high-fashion designers, prestigious fashion weeks, and the chance to become the face of luxury brands.

2. Print Modeling:
- Stills and Photography: Print models feature in various print media, including magazines, catalogs, advertisements, and online campaigns. This niche encompasses a wide range of styles, from fashion to commercial to editorial.
- Diverse Requirements: Print modeling is more inclusive in terms of height and measurements, making it accessible to a broader range of individuals.
- Opportunities: Print models have the opportunity to work with diverse clients, from fashion magazines to lifestyle brands, and can build a diverse portfolio.
3. Specialty Modeling:
- Niche Specialization: Specialty models focus on specific areas like hand modeling, hair modeling, jewelry modeling, fitness modeling, and more. These niches require unique attributes or skills.
- Varied Requirements: Specialized niches have distinct requirements. For instance, hand models should have well-groomed hands, while fitness models need to maintain a fit physique.

- Opportunities: Specialty models cater to niche markets and often find success in industries like beauty, fitness, and product promotion.

CHOOSING YOUR NICHE
Here are steps to help you select the modeling niche that suits you best:

1. Self-Assessment: Reflect on your physical attributes, skills, and interests. What are your strengths, and what niche complements them? Consider your height, measurements, and unique features.

2. Research: Learn about the various modeling niches in detail. Study the requirements, expectations, and opportunities associated with each one.

3. Consult Industry Professionals: Seek advice from experienced models or industry professionals. They can provide valuable insights and guidance based on their experiences.

4. Test the Waters: Experiment with different modeling opportunities. Attend open calls, portfolio-building sessions, and casting calls in various niches to gain firsthand experience.

5. Consult with Agencies: If you're represented by a modeling agency, discuss your niche options with them. Agencies can help you identify your strengths and guide your career path.

NICHE MODELING TIPS AND TRICKS
- Diversity: Don't limit yourself to one niche if you have the versatility to excel in multiple areas. Expanding your repertoire can open doors to more opportunities.
- Adaptability: Be open to adapting your modeling style based on the client's needs. Flexibility can help you thrive in a dynamic industry.
- Portfolio Building: Develop a portfolio that showcases your skills in your chosen niche. Your portfolio is your visual resume, so make it compelling.
- Networking: Connect with professionals in your niche. Attend niche-specific events, workshops, and conventions to expand your network.

Choosing your modeling niche is a significant step in your modeling career. It's a decision that should align with your unique qualities and career goals. Whether you're strutting down runways, gracing magazine covers, or specializing in a niche market, remember that modeling is a diverse and ever-evolving field. Embrace the niche that resonates with you the most and be prepared to adapt and grow as your modeling journey unfolds. Your niche is your canvas; it's time to paint your modeling masterpiece.

MODELING NICHE: RUNWAY, PRINT, OR BEYOND

In the competitive world of modeling, identifying and capitalizing on your unique strengths is essential for building a successful career. Your strengths set you apart, attract clients, and define your niche within the industry. In this chapter, we'll delve into the process of discovering your modeling strengths to propel your career forward.

1. Self-Reflection and Assessment
Begin your journey of discovering your modeling strengths with self-reflection and honest self-assessment. Consider the following aspects:
- Physical Attributes: Reflect on your height, body type, facial features, and any distinctive characteristics. What physical attributes make you stand out?
- Skills and Talents: Identify any specialized skills or talents that can enhance your modeling career. This might include dancing, acting, or a proficiency in certain sports.
- Comfort Zone: Assess where you feel most comfortable and confident. Are you at ease on the runway, in front of the camera, or in specific niche markets?
- Interests and Passions: Consider your interests and passions outside of modeling. Do they align with certain modeling niches, such as fitness, fashion, or lifestyle?

2. Seek Feedback and Guidance
Engage with industry professionals, such as modeling agents, photographers, and experienced models, to gain valuable

feedback and insights. They can provide an external perspective on your strengths and areas for improvement.
- Modeling Agencies: If you're represented by a modeling agency, consult with your agent. They have experience matching models with suitable opportunities based on their strengths.
- Photographers: Photographers work closely with models and can offer feedback on your posing, expressions, and overall presence in front of the camera.
- Peer Feedback: Connect with fellow models. They can provide peer feedback and share their observations about your modeling strengths.

3. Portfolio Analysis
Examine your modeling portfolio critically. Your portfolio is a visual representation of your work and can reveal patterns in your strengths and preferences.
- Diverse Portfolio: Analyze the types of jobs and projects you've excelled in. Identify recurring themes or styles that align with your strengths.
- Client Feedback: Consider any positive feedback or testimonials you've received from clients and photographers. Their comments can highlight your strengths.

4. Experiment and Explore
Don't be afraid to explore various modeling opportunities and niches. Sometimes, your modeling strengths may emerge

as you gain experience in different settings.
- Test Shoots: Collaborate with photographers and stylists on test shoots to experiment with different styles and concepts.
- Niche Modeling: Try modeling in various niches, from fashion and commercial to fitness and editorial. You may discover a niche where your strengths truly shine.

5. Embrace Versatility
While it's crucial to identify your strengths, also embrace versatility. Being adaptable and open to new experiences can enhance your modeling career.
- Training: Invest in modeling training and workshops to refine your skills and broaden your capabilities.
- Portfolio Expansion: Continuously update and expand your portfolio to showcase your evolving strengths and versatility.

6. Stay Informed
Keep yourself informed about the latest trends, market demands, and emerging niches within the modeling industry. Staying current can help you identify new opportunities that align with your strengths.

7. Seek Professional Guidance
If you're uncertain about your modeling strengths or career direction, consider seeking guidance from a career counselor or modeling coach. They can provide objective insights and help you formulate a career strategy.

Discovering your modeling strengths is a dynamic and ongoing process. It involves self-reflection, seeking feedback, analyzing your portfolio, experimenting with different opportunities, and staying adaptable. Embrace your strengths, leverage them to build a standout career, and remember that your unique qualities are your ticket to success in the world of modeling. As you uncover your strengths, you'll not only excel in your modeling career but also find fulfillment in showcasing your authentic self to the world.

6

PREPARING FOR A CASTING CALL

A casting call is your opportunity to impress potential clients, agencies, or designers and secure modeling jobs. How you prepare for a casting can significantly impact your chances of success. In this chapter, we'll guide you through the essential steps to prepare effectively for a casting.

1. Research the Casting
Before attending any casting, it's crucial to gather information about the event, client, or project. Here's what you should consider:
- Client or Company: Research the client or company holding the casting. Familiarize yourself with their style, brand, and previous work. Understanding their aesthetic can help you tailor your presentation.
- Casting Details: Know the date, time, and location of the

casting. Ensure you arrive punctually, as being late can leave a negative impression.
- Casting Requirements: Understand the specific requirements for the casting. This could include age, height, body type, hair color, or other criteria.

2. Create a Strong Portfolio
Your portfolio is your visual resume, showcasing your range and versatility as a model. Ensure your portfolio is up-to-date and tailored to the casting's needs.
- Select Appropriate Photos: Choose portfolio images that align with the casting's requirements and style. For instance, if it's a high-fashion casting, emphasize your high-fashion work.
- Variety: Include a variety of shots, including headshots, full-body shots, and different styles (e.g., fashion, commercial, editorial).

3. Dress Appropriately
Your clothing should reflect the casting's requirements and the client's brand. Here are some tips:
- Wear Simple, Fitted Clothing: Choose simple, well-fitted attire that complements your body type. Avoid clothing with logos or patterns that may distract.
- Nude-Colored Undergarments: Opt for nude-colored undergarments to avoid visible lines under clothing.

- High Heels: If the casting requires heels, bring a pair that you're comfortable walking in. Ensure your walk is confident and natural in heels.

4. Grooming and Makeup
Your appearance should be clean, polished, and in line with the casting's expectations. Here's what to consider:
- Basic Makeup: Keep makeup natural and subtle. A clean, well-maintained appearance is often preferred.
- Hair: Style your hair neatly. If you have long hair, bring hair ties in case the casting requires you to tie it back.
- Nails: Ensure your nails are well-groomed and clean. Neutral nail polish is a safe choice.

5. Bring Essentials
Pack a modeling toolkit with essential items:
- Comp Card: Bring several copies of your comp card to leave with the casting team.
- Resume: Include a modeling resume detailing your experience and previous work.
- Identification: Carry a valid ID, such as a driver's license or passport.
- Pen and Notebook: These are handy for taking notes or filling out casting forms.
- Snacks and Water: Have a small snack and a bottle of water on hand for sustenance.

6. Practice Your Introduction
Prepare a brief, professional introduction that includes your
name, agency (if applicable), and a warm greeting. Practice it
to ensure confidence and clarity.

7. Confidence and Professionalism
Confidence is key during a casting. Project professionalism
and a positive attitude:
- Confident Walk: If asked to walk, maintain a confident and
natural runway walk.
- Be Polite: Be polite and respectful to everyone you interact
with at the casting, including other models, casting directors,
and staff.

8. Be Prepared to Take Direction
During the casting, the client or casting director may provide
specific instructions or ask you to demonstrate different
poses or expressions. Not only should you be receptive to
feedback and direction but make sure you follow the
directions exactly as they are given to you. An ability to follow
precise directions indicates how it will be to work with you.

9. Follow Up
After the casting, consider sending a brief thank-you email or
message to express your gratitude for the opportunity. This
can leave a positive impression and demonstrate your
professionalism. Do not email repeatedly as to if you were
selected.

PREPARING FOR A CASTING CALL

Preparing for a casting is a crucial step in securing modeling jobs. Research, preparation, and professionalism are your allies in making a lasting impression. Remember that each casting experience is an opportunity to learn and grow in your modeling career, regardless of the outcome. Stay persistent, stay positive, and you'll be well-prepared to succeed in the competitive world of modeling.

7

BEYOND THE BASICS: HAIR & MAKEUP

Your hair and makeup play a significant role in your overall presentation during casting calls. Casting directors often look for a clean, versatile look that allows them to envision you in various roles or styles. In this chapter, we'll guide you through the process of styling your hair and makeup for casting calls.

1. KEEP IT NATURAL
The key to successful hair and makeup for castings is to appear natural and fresh-faced. Casting directors want to see your true appearance, so avoid heavy or dramatic looks. Here's how to achieve a natural look:
For Makeup:
- Skin: Begin with a clean, well-moisturized face. Use a lightweight foundation or tinted moisturizer to even out your skin tone.

BEYOND THE BASICS: HAIR & MAKEUP

- Eyes: Stick to neutral eyeshadows in shades like beige, taupe, or soft brown. Avoid heavy eyeliner or dramatic eyeshadow.
- Lashes: Use mascara to define your lashes without making them overly dramatic. Skip false lashes for castings.
- Lips: Choose a nude or light pink lip color. Avoid bold or bright lipsticks.
- Brows: Groom your eyebrows neatly with a brow gel or pencil if necessary. Keep them looking natural and well-maintained.

For Hair:
- Clean and Healthy: Ensure your hair is clean and well-groomed. Clean, healthy hair always makes a positive impression.
- Simple Styles: Opt for simple hairstyles that don't distract from your face. A neat bun, ponytail, or loose waves can work well.
- Avoid Elaborate Updos: Elaborate updos or hairstyles with excessive accessories should be avoided. Casting directors want to see your natural hair texture.

2. NEUTRAL COLORS

When choosing makeup colors, stick to neutral tones that enhance your natural features without overpowering them. Neutral shades for eyeshadows, blush, and lip colors are ideal.

3. MINIMAL PRODUCTS

Avoid overloading your face with makeup products. The goal is to create a fresh, clean canvas. Using too many products can appear heavy and unnatural.

4. FLAWLESS SKIN

Focus on achieving flawless-looking skin. Use concealer to cover blemishes or under-eye circles if needed. Set your makeup with a light dusting of translucent powder to reduce shine.

5. PRACTICE YOUR LOOK

Before a casting, practice your natural makeup look and hairstyle to ensure you can recreate it quickly and effortlessly on the day of the casting.

6. MAINTAIN YOUR APPEARANCE

During the casting, periodically check your makeup and hair to ensure everything remains in place. Carry a small kit with essentials like blotting papers, concealer, and lip balm for touch-ups if necessary.

7. HYDRATION AND SKINCARE

Leading up to the casting, prioritize hydration and skincare. Well-moisturized skin provides a better canvas for makeup application.

8. CONSULT WITH PROFESSIONALS

If you're unsure about achieving a natural look on your own, consider consulting with a professional makeup artist and hairstylist. They can provide guidance and help you create a simple, natural look.

9. BE PREPARED FOR CHANGES

Casting directors may request specific looks or hairstyles during the casting. Be open to making quick adjustments if needed.

Styling your hair and makeup for casting calls should emphasize your natural beauty while maintaining a clean and versatile appearance. The goal is to allow casting directors to see your potential for various roles. With the right approach, you can present yourself in the best light and increase your chances of making a memorable impression during castings.

8

HEALTHY FITNESS & NUTRITION

Maintaining a healthy lifestyle is paramount for models. It not only enhances your appearance but also supports your overall well-being and longevity in the industry. In this chapter, we'll explore fitness and nutrition habits that can help models stay in top shape and feel their best.

1. PRIORITIZE BALANCED NUTRITION
Nutrition is the foundation of a healthy lifestyle. Proper nutrition can help you maintain optimal energy levels, healthy skin, and a fit physique. Here are some key principles to follow:
- Balanced Diet: Consume a well-rounded diet that includes a variety of fruits, vegetables, lean proteins, whole grains, and healthy fats.
- Hydration: Stay adequately hydrated by drinking plenty of water throughout the day. Dehydration can affect your skin and overall health.

- Portion Control: Be mindful of portion sizes to prevent overeating. Pay attention to your body's hunger and fullness cues.
- Limit Processed Foods: Minimize your intake of processed and sugary foods, which can lead to energy crashes and skin issues.

2. PLAN MEALS AND SNACKS
For models with busy schedules, planning meals and snacks is crucial to ensure you're nourishing your body consistently. Here's how to approach meal planning:
- Regular Eating Schedule: Aim to eat every 3-4 hours to maintain stable energy levels and prevent overeating later in the day.
- Healthy Snacks: Keep healthy snacks like nuts, fruits, and yogurt on hand for quick, nutritious options between meals.
- Meal Prep: Consider meal prepping for the week to have balanced, homemade meals readily available.

3. FOCUS ON SKIN HEALTH
Your skin is a significant asset as a model. To maintain healthy, glowing skin, consider the following:
- Skincare Routine: Establish a daily skincare routine that includes cleansing, moisturizing, and sun protection. Consult with a dermatologist for personalized skincare advice.
- Avoid Overexposure: Protect your skin from excessive sun exposure, which can lead to premature aging and skin damage.

- Adequate Sleep: Do not underestimate how important a healthy sleep schedule is to your overall fitness. Ensure you get enough sleep, as it's crucial for skin repair and rejuvenation.

4. EMBRACE REGULAR EXERCISE

Regular physical activity helps you maintain a toned physique, enhance flexibility, and boost your overall health. Here's how to incorporate exercise into your routine:
- Varied Workouts: Engage in a variety of workouts, including cardiovascular exercises, strength training, and flexibility exercises like yoga or pilates.
- Consistency: Aim for consistency in your exercise routine. Schedule workouts that align with your availability.
- Consult a Trainer: Consider working with a fitness trainer to create a tailored exercise plan that meets your modeling goals.

5. MANAGE STRESS EFFECTIVELY

Modeling can be demanding, both physically and mentally. Stress management is essential for maintaining overall health. Strategies to manage stress include:
- Mindfulness and Meditation: Practice mindfulness techniques or meditation to reduce stress and promote mental clarity.
- Time Management: Use effective time management strategies to balance work and personal life.

- Seek Support: Don't hesitate to seek support from a therapist or counselor if you're dealing with stress or mental health issues.

6. REGULAR HEALTH CHECKUPS
Regular medical checkups are crucial for identifying and addressing health issues early. Schedule routine appointments with your healthcare provider, including dermatologists and nutritionists, to maintain your well-being.

7. AVOID EXTREME DIETS OR TRENDS
Extreme diets or weight loss trends can be detrimental to your health and may not provide sustainable results. Focus on long-term, healthy eating habits instead.

8. LISTEN TO YOUR BODY
Pay attention to your body's signals. If you're feeling fatigued, unwell, or stressed, it's essential to listen to your body and take the necessary steps to address these issues. Maintaining a healthy lifestyle is fundamental for models. By prioritizing balanced nutrition, regular exercise, skin health, stress management, and overall well-being, you can not only look your best but also feel your best. A healthy model is a successful and confident one, ready to conquer the demanding world of fashion and modeling with grace and vitality.

9

CRAFTING A STELLAR PORTFOLIO

Your modeling portfolio is your calling card, your visual resume, and your chance to make a memorable first impression in the industry. A stellar portfolio is not just about having a collection of beautiful photos; it's about demonstrating your versatility, adaptability, and range as a model. In this chapter, we'll explore what makes a portfolio exceptional and why content from different situations is key to your success.

1. WHY A STELLAR PORTFOLIO MATTERS
A stellar portfolio is your most powerful tool as a model. It serves several essential functions:
- First Impression: Casting directors, agencies, and clients often make quick judgments based on your portfolio. It's your opportunity to capture their attention.

- Showcasing Abilities: Your portfolio showcases your skills, versatility, and range. It demonstrates your ability to adapt to various styles, settings, and concepts.
- Marketing Tool: It's a marketing tool that can attract clients and bookings. A strong portfolio can lead to more opportunities and higher-paying jobs.

2. THE ROLE OF DIVERSE CONTENT
Diversity in your portfolio is essential for several reasons:
- Versatility: Diverse content highlights your versatility as a model. It shows that you can excel in a wide range of styles, from high fashion to commercial work.
- Adaptability: It demonstrates your adaptability in different situations and settings. Clients want to know that you can perform well under various conditions.
- Audience Connection: Diverse content allows you to connect with a broader audience. People from different backgrounds and preferences should see themselves in your work.
Tip: Take advantage of content events where you can secure images you can use from professional photographers.

3. TYPES OF DIVERSE CONTENT
To create a stellar portfolio, consider including content from various situations:
- Fashion: High-fashion shots that demonstrate your ability to wear and carry luxury clothing and accessories.

- Commercial: Commercial modeling for everyday products or services, showing relatability and approachability.
- Editorial: Editorial work that tells a story, conveys a message, or evokes emotion. This demonstrates your storytelling abilities.
- Lifestyle: Images that depict a specific lifestyle or activity, such as fitness, travel, or beauty.
- Cultural: Content that embraces different cultures and ethnicities, making your portfolio more inclusive and relatable.
- Niche: Specialized content if you're pursuing niche modeling like hand modeling, fitness modeling, or plus-size modeling.

4. QUALITY OVER QUANTITY
While diversity is crucial, remember that the quality of your portfolio content is paramount. It's better to have a smaller selection of outstanding images than a large collection of mediocre ones.
- Choose the Best: Be selective in choosing the images that truly represent your best work and your range as a model.
- Regular Updates: Regularly update your portfolio to reflect your growth, new experiences, and the evolution of your skills.

5. COLLABORATIONS AND TEAMWORK
Collaboration is often the key to diverse content. Work with skilled photographers, makeup artists, stylists, and other

professionals to create compelling images.
- Networking: Build relationships with industry professionals who can help you expand your portfolio.
- Conceptualization: Collaborate on creative concepts that challenge your abilities and showcase your uniqueness.

6. TELL YOUR STORY
Your portfolio should tell a story about who you are as a model. Let it reflect your personality, your passions, and your journey.
- Consistency: Maintain a consistent theme or style that represents your brand as a model.
- Evolution: Show your growth and progression over time. Let viewers see how you've honed your craft.

A stellar portfolio is your passport to success in the modeling world. By emphasizing the importance of content from different situations and showcasing your versatility and adaptability, you can make a lasting impression and open doors to a wide range of modeling opportunities. Your portfolio should be a dynamic reflection of your unique talents and your ability to shine in any situation or style.

10

AGENCIES & FREELANCING

UNDERSTANDING THE PROS AND CONS
One of the most significant decisions you'll make as a model is whether to work with a modeling agency or pursue a freelancing career. Each path has its advantages and drawbacks, and the choice depends on your goals, personality, and circumstances. In this chapter, we'll explore the key differences between working with agencies and freelancing, along with the pros and cons of each option.

WORKING WITH A MODELING AGENCY

Pros:
1. Industry Expertise: Agencies have extensive industry knowledge and connections. They can guide your career and provide valuable insights.

2. Access to Opportunities: Agencies have access to a broad range of job opportunities, including high-profile gigs and international assignments.

3. Professional Guidance: Experienced agents can offer professional guidance, helping you navigate contracts, negotiate rates, and manage your career effectively.

4. Steady Work: Established agencies often have a consistent stream of work, providing financial stability for models.

5. Brand Credibility: Being associated with a reputable agency can enhance your credibility and make it easier to secure bookings.

Cons:
1. Agency Commission: Agencies typically deduct a commission (usually 10-20%) from your earnings, reducing your take-home pay.

2. Loss of Control: You may have limited control over the jobs you accept, as agencies make decisions on your behalf.

3. Competitive Environment: Agencies represent multiple models, so competition within the agency can be fierce.

4. Contractual Obligations: Agency contracts may come with

exclusivity clauses or other restrictions that limit your freelancing opportunities.

5. Initial Investment: Some agencies may require upfront fees for services like portfolio development or marketing.

FREELANCING AS A MODEL

Pros:
1. Independence: Freelancing offers greater control over your career. You can choose the projects you take on and manage your own schedule.

2. Higher Earnings: Without agency commissions, you may earn more per booking.

3. Diverse Opportunities: You can explore a wide range of modeling opportunities, from fashion to niche markets, without agency limitations.

4. Networking: Freelancing encourages direct client interactions, enabling you to build valuable relationships in the industry.

5. Personal Brand: You have the freedom to build and promote your personal brand, which can lead to unique opportunities.

Cons:

1. Self-Promotion: Freelancers must handle their own marketing, self-promotion, and networking, which can be time-consuming.

2. Uncertainty: Freelancing can be financially uncertain, with irregular bookings and income fluctuations.

3. No Safety Net: You won't have the support system provided by an agency, such as career guidance, portfolio development, and legal assistance.

4. Competition: Freelance modeling is highly competitive, as you're responsible for securing your own clients and jobs.

5. Administrative Tasks: You'll need to manage administrative tasks like invoicing, contracts, and tax obligations.

MAKING THE DECISION

Choosing between working with an agency and freelancing depends on your career goals, personality, and circumstances. Some models start with agencies to gain experience and then transition to freelancing, while others thrive in agency settings throughout their careers. It's essential to assess your priorities, consider the pros and cons, and make an informed decision that aligns with your vision for your modeling career.

Remember that there's no one-size-fits-all answer, and your path may evolve over time. Whichever path you choose, success in the modeling industry ultimately comes down to your dedication, professionalism, and commitment to honing your craft.

11

NAVIGATING THE FASHION INDUSTRY

Entering the fashion industry as a professional model is an exciting and rewarding journey. However, it's essential to understand the intricacies of the industry to succeed. In this chapter, we'll explore the key aspects of navigating the fashion industry as a professional model.

UNDERSTANDING THE FASHION INDUSTRY
1. Fashion Hierarchy: The fashion industry operates on a hierarchy, with various segments like high fashion, commercial, and niche markets. Know where you fit and where you want to excel.

2. Fashion Seasons: Fashion operates on seasons (spring/summer and fall/winter). Understanding these cycles is crucial, as it impacts when and where you'll be working.

3. Fashion Capitals: Major cities like New York, Paris, Milan, and London are fashion capitals. These cities host prominent fashion weeks and offer extensive modeling opportunities.

BUILDING YOUR BRAND
1. Personal Branding: Develop a strong personal brand that reflects your unique style and personality. Your brand sets you apart and attracts specific clients and opportunities.

2. Portfolio Development: Continually update and improve your portfolio with high-quality images that showcase your versatility and range as a model.

NETWORKING AND PROFESSIONALISM
1. Networking: Building relationships in the industry is essential. Attend a myriad of industry events, collaborate with professionals, and connect with photographers, designers, and other models.

2. Professionalism: Maintain a professional demeanor at all times. Punctuality, reliability, and a positive attitude are key to building a good reputation.

MODELING AGENCIES
1. Choosing an Agency: If you work with an agency, select one that aligns with your goals and values. Read contracts carefully, and don't hesitate to ask questions.

2. Contracts: Understand your agency contract thoroughly. Be aware of exclusivity clauses, commissions, and other terms.

FASHION SHOWS AND RUNWAY
1. Fashion Weeks: Familiarize yourself with the fashion weeks in major cities. These events are critical for runway models.

2. Runway Techniques: Practice your runway walk regularly. Master different styles, from high fashion struts to commercial walks.

EDITORIAL AND PRINT MODELING
1. Posing: Hone your posing skills to convey emotion and storytelling through your images.

2. Magazine Submissions: Collaborate with photographers and stylists to submit your work to magazines. Getting published enhances your visibility.

COMMERCIAL MODELING
1. Auditions: Attend commercial auditions and casting calls for advertising campaigns, television commercials, and other commercial work.

2. Relatability: Commercial models need to appear relatable and approachable. Adapt to various roles and scenarios.

SELF-CARE AND WELLNESS
1. Health: Prioritize your physical and mental health. Maintain a balanced diet, exercise, and manage stress effectively.

2. Skin and Hair: Skincare and haircare routines are essential. A flawless appearance is critical in the fashion industry.

LEGAL CONSIDERATIONS
1. Contracts: Seek legal advice when dealing with contracts. Understand your rights, responsibilities, and potential legal implications.

2. Model Release Forms: When participating in photoshoots, ensure you understand the terms of the model release form, which governs how your images will be used.

CONTINUOUS LEARNING
1. Education: Never stop learning about the industry. Attend workshops, take classes, and stay informed about fashion trends and industry changes.

2. Feedback: Be open to feedback from industry professionals. Constructive criticism can help you improve your craft.

Navigating the fashion industry as a professional model requires dedication, adaptability, and a commitment to

NAVIGATING THE FASHION INDUSTRY

continuous improvement. Stay true to your brand, build strong relationships, and approach each opportunity with professionalism and enthusiasm. With the right mindset and preparation, you can make a lasting mark in the dynamic and exciting world of fashion modeling.

12

THE IMPORTANCE OF NETWORKING

Networking is a fundamental aspect of building a successful career in the fashion industry. As a professional model, your ability to connect with others, build relationships, and create a network of industry contacts can significantly impact your opportunities and long-term success. In this chapter, we'll delve into the importance of networking and provide strategies to enhance your networking skills.

Why Networking Matters

1. Access to Opportunities: Networking provides access to a vast array of opportunities. You'll learn about casting calls, job openings, and projects that may not be publicly advertised.

2. Career Growth: Building a network can help you progress in

your career. Industry professionals you connect with today may become your collaborators, agents, or clients in the future.

3. Knowledge Sharing: Networking allows you to learn from others' experiences and gain valuable insights into the industry. You can exchange tips, advice, and industry trends with peers and mentors.

4. Support System: A strong network can be a source of emotional support and camaraderie. It's helpful to connect with people who understand the unique challenges and demands of the fashion industry.

5. Diverse Collaborations: Networking exposes you to a diverse range of collaborators. You can work with photographers, designers, makeup artists, and stylists who contribute to your portfolio and skillset.

TIPS FOR EFFECTIVE NETWORKING STRATEGIES
1. Attend Industry Events: Fashion shows, industry mixers, fashion weeks, and trade shows are excellent places to meet. Be proactive and introduce yourself to others.

2. Online Platforms: Utilize social media platforms like Instagram, LinkedIn, and professional websites to showcase your work and connect with industry peers. Engage in meaningful conversations and collaborations.

3. Collaborate on Projects: Collaborative projects are an excellent way to build your network. Partner with photographers, makeup artists, and stylists for photoshoots and creative projects.

4. Mentorship: Seek out mentors in the industry who can offer guidance and support. Mentorship relationships can provide valuable insights and open doors to new opportunities.

5. Professional Organizations: Join professional organizations or associations related to modeling and fashion. These groups often host networking events and provide resources for career development.

6. Be Reliable and Professional: Reputation matters in the fashion industry. Be punctual, reliable, and maintain professionalism in your interactions.

7. Follow Up: After meeting someone in the industry, follow up with a polite email or message. Express your interest in maintaining the connection and inquire about potential collaborations.

8. Give Back: Offer your assistance or expertise to others when possible. Generosity within your network can lead to reciprocity and strengthen relationships.

THE IMPORTANCE OF NETWORKING

MAINTAINING YOUR NETWORK
Building a network is valuable, but maintaining it is equally important. Here are tips for nurturing and sustaining your industry connections:

1. Regular Communication: Stay in touch with your network regularly. Send updates on your work, congratulate them on their achievements, and share relevant industry news.

2. Attend Reunions: Participate in reunions, industry events, and gatherings. These occasions offer opportunities to reconnect and strengthen bonds.

3. Offer Help: Be willing to assist your network when they need it. Whether it's providing referrals, collaborating on projects, or offering advice, your support can solidify relationships.

4. Express Gratitude: Don't forget to express your gratitude. Thank those who have helped you along the way and acknowledge the positive impact they've had on your career.

5. Adapt and Evolve: The fashion industry is dynamic. Stay adaptable and open to change. Your network can help you stay informed about industry shifts and trends.

12
THE IMPORTANCE OF NETWORKING

Networking is a cornerstone of success in the fashion industry. By actively building and maintaining a strong network of industry professionals, you can access opportunities, gain insights, and forge meaningful collaborations that propel your modeling career to new heights. Remember that networking is an ongoing process, and the relationships you cultivate today can lead to exciting possibilities in the future.

13

HANDLING REJECTION *&* MAINTAINING CONFIDENCE

Rejection is an inevitable part of a modeling career. In an industry where competition is fierce and subjective opinions prevail, it's essential to develop resilience and maintain your self-confidence despite setbacks. In this chapter, we'll explore strategies for handling rejection and preserving your self-assuredness as a professional model.

UNDERSTANDING REJECTION
1. Subjectivity: Recognize that the fashion and modeling industry is highly subjective. Casting decisions often depend on the vision of photographers, designers, and clients.

2. Numbers Game: Even successful models face rejection regularly. Rejection isn't a reflection of your worth or talent but a natural aspect of the profession.

HANDLING REJECTION *&* MAINTAINING CONFIDENCE

3. Growth Opportunity: View rejection as an opportunity for growth. Each experience can teach you something valuable about your craft and your personal resilience.

STRATEGIES FOR HANDLING REJECTION

1. Maintain Perspective: Keep the bigger picture in mind. One rejection does not define your entire career. Focus on your long-term goals and the progress you've made.

2. Self-Reflection: After a rejection, take time to self-reflect. Assess your performance objectively and identify areas for improvement.

3. Positive Self-Talk: Practice positive self-talk. Replace self-criticism with affirmations and reminders of your achievements and strengths.

4. Seek Feedback: When appropriate, ask for feedback from industry professionals. Constructive criticism can help you identify areas to work on.

5. Embrace Resilience: Cultivate resilience as a core skill. Resilient individuals bounce back from setbacks, adapt to challenges, and remain motivated.

6. Support System: Lean on your support system. Share your experiences and feelings with friends, family, or mentors who can provide emotional support.

HANDLING REJECTION *&* MAINTAINING CONFIDENCE

7. Learn and Grow: Use rejection as a catalyst for growth. Consider taking workshops or classes to refine your skills and expand your portfolio.

MAINTAINING CONFIDENCE
1. Positive Self-Image: Develop a healthy self-image. Recognize and embrace your unique qualities that set you apart in the industry.

2. Self-Care: Prioritize self-care practices that promote physical and mental well-being. Exercise, a balanced diet, and mindfulness activities can boost confidence.

3. Confidence Building Exercises: Engage in confidence-building exercises, such as visualizing success, setting achievable goals, and celebrating your accomplishments.

4. Modeling Experience: Draw confidence from your modeling experience. Remind yourself of the successful projects and bookings you've achieved.

5. Supportive Network: Surround yourself with a supportive network of professionals and peers who believe in your potential.

6. Personal Brand: Continuously work on building and reinforcing your personal brand. Confidence is an attractive quality in the fashion industry.

7. Professionalism: Maintain professionalism in all your interactions. Confidence often stems from a sense of competence and capability.

DEALING WITH PERSISTENT REJECTION
In some cases, rejection may persist despite your best efforts. It's essential to recognize when it's time to reevaluate your approach or seek guidance:

1. Self-Assessment: Assess if your goals align with the market and your capabilities. Be open to exploring different modeling niches.

2. Mentorship: Consider seeking mentorship from experienced models or industry professionals. They can offer insights and guidance.

3. Agent or Agency Discussion: If you work with an agency, discuss your concerns with your agent. They can provide guidance and help you navigate the industry.

4. Evaluate Your Portfolio: Regularly assess your portfolio. Ensure it accurately represents your versatility and marketability.

5. Market Research: Stay informed about industry trends and market demands. Adapting to changing preferences may increase your success rate.

HANDLING REJECTION & MAINTAINING CONFIDENCE

Handling rejection and maintaining confidence are essential skills for a professional model. Remember that rejection is a natural part of the industry and does not define your worth. By adopting strategies to cope with rejection, preserving your self-confidence, and continuously working on your personal and professional growth, you can thrive in the competitive world of modeling while staying true to yourself. Your journey may have its ups and downs, but each experience contributes to your growth and resilience as a model.

14

INTERNATIONAL MODELING & TRAVELING TIPS

International modeling opportunities can be incredibly exciting and rewarding, offering the chance to work in diverse markets and collaborate with professionals from around the world. However, modeling abroad also comes with unique challenges and considerations. In this chapter, we'll explore the ins and outs of international modeling and provide essential tips for navigating this thrilling aspect of your career.

PREPARING FOR INTERNATIONAL MODELING
1. Market Research: Research the international modeling markets you're interested in. Understand the local fashion scene, industry norms, and the types of models in demand.

2. Visa and Work Permits: Ensure you have the necessary visas and work permits to legally work in your destination country.

Start this process well in advance.

3. Agency Representation: Consider seeking representation with a local agency in your destination country. They can assist with bookings, legal requirements, and local insights.

4. Travel Documentation: Keep copies of essential documents, including your passport, visa, modeling portfolio, and any legal contracts. Share these copies with a trusted person in case of emergencies.

TRAVELING TIPS
1. Packing Essentials: Pack your modeling essentials, including a versatile wardrobe, comfortable shoes, grooming products, and professional accessories. Consider any specific requirements for your destination.

2. Health Precautions: Research any required vaccinations or health precautions for your destination. Carry necessary medications and prescriptions.

3. Local Currency: Familiarize yourself with the local currency and have some cash on hand for emergencies. Notify your bank of your travel plans to avoid card issues.

4. Communication: Invest in a reliable international phone plan or local SIM card to stay connected. Download translation apps for ease of communication.

ON ARRIVAL

1. Orientation: Get acquainted with your new surroundings. Know the locations of your agency, casting venues, and important services like hospitals and embassies.

2. Network Locally: Attend industry events, fashion weeks, and networking functions to connect with local professionals and models. Building local relationships can lead to more opportunities.

3. Cultural Sensitivity: Respect local customs and traditions, both in and out of work. Understanding cultural nuances will help you navigate social situations professionally.

WORKING INTERNATIONALLY

1. Language Skills: If possible, learn basic phrases in the local language. This can improve communication and demonstrate your commitment to the local market.

2. Contracts and Agreements: Read and understand any contracts or agreements thoroughly, including payment terms, usage rights, and any exclusivity clauses. Adjust your schedule gradually to adapt to the local time zone.

3. Travel Insurance: Invest in comprehensive travel insurance that covers health emergencies, lost luggage, and trip cancellations.

STAYING SAFE

1. Safety Precautions: Stay in secure accommodations, and avoid traveling alone at night. Keep your belongings secure, especially in crowded areas.

2. Emergency Contacts: Share your itinerary and contact information with someone you trust back home. Provide them with updates on your whereabouts.

HEALTH AND WELL-BEING

1. Maintain Health: Prioritize your health by getting enough sleep, staying hydrated, and eating balanced meals. Travel and work can be demanding, so self-care is crucial.

2. Jet Lag: Combat jet lag with proper rest and hydration.

RETURNING HOME

1. Review and Reflect: Take time to reflect on your international experience. Assess your successes, challenges, and lessons learned for future travels.

2. Settle Finances: Attend to any financial matters, such as tax obligations, currency exchange, and banking.

International modeling can be a thrilling and enriching experience that broadens your horizons and expands your career. By preparing diligently, staying informed, respecting local customs, and prioritizing your well-being, you can make the most of your international opportunities while ensuring a safe and successful journey. Embrace the adventure, and let each international assignment contribute to your growth and expertise as a professional model.

15

LEGAL & ETHICAL CONSIDERATIONS

Navigating the legal and ethical aspects of the modeling industry is essential to protect your rights, reputation, and career. In this chapter, we'll explore key legal and ethical considerations that professional models should be aware of, including essential information about photo copyright rules when posting images on social media. This is not legal advice. Consult an attorney for specific information and guidance.

MODEL RELEASE FORMS
Model release forms are crucial legal documents in the modeling industry. These forms grant permission for the use of your likeness in photographs or videos. Here's what you need to know:

1. Purpose: Model release forms are used to obtain your consent for the use and distribution of your images by

photographers, agencies, and clients. This consent is essential for commercial and promotional purposes.

2. Content: A typical model release form includes your name, signature, the date of the agreement, and details about how the images will be used. Be sure to read the form carefully before signing it.

3. Rights: Model release forms may specify whether you are granting exclusive or non-exclusive rights for image usage. Exclusive rights restrict your ability to work with other brands or agencies using similar content.

4. Revocability: Once you sign a model release form, it is typically not revocable. Ensure you are comfortable with the terms before providing your consent.

COPYRIGHT RULES AND SOCIAL MEDIA
Posting images on social media is a common practice for models to showcase their work and engage with their audience. However, there are important copyright considerations to keep in mind:

1. Ownership: Photographers typically own the copyright to the images they capture, even if you are the subject. It's essential to respect their rights and seek permission before posting or using these images.

LEGAL & ETHICAL CONSIDERATIONS

2. Credit and Attribution: Always credit the photographer when sharing their work on social media. This not only shows respect for their creativity but also helps clarify copyright ownership.

3. License Agreements: In some cases, photographers may grant you specific usage rights or licenses for social media. Read and adhere to these agreements carefully.

4. Model Release Forms: Ensure that the use of images on social media aligns with the terms specified in your model release forms. Violating these terms could have legal consequences.

5. Public vs. Private: Consider your privacy settings on social media platforms. Posting publicly may expose your images to a wider audience, while private settings restrict access.

6. Professionalism: Maintain professionalism in your social media posts. Avoid posting controversial or inappropriate content that could negatively impact your career.

ETHICAL CONSIDERATIONS
Ethical considerations are equally important in maintaining a reputable modeling career:

LEGAL & ETHICAL CONSIDERATIONS

1. Honest Representation: Represent yourself accurately. Don't mislead clients or agencies with manipulated or heavily edited images.

2. Professional Behavior: Uphold professionalism in all interactions with colleagues, clients, and industry professionals. Be punctual, reliable, and respectful.

3. Respect Boundaries: Set and respect personal boundaries during photoshoots and engagements. Never be afraid to communicate openly with photographers and clients about your comfort levels.

4. Diversity and Inclusion: Promote diversity and inclusion in the industry. Encourage fair representation of all backgrounds and body types.

5. Advocacy: Use your platform to advocate for ethical and social causes that align with your values.

LEGAL PROTECTIONS
Understanding your legal rights and protections is crucial:

1. Contracts: Review all contracts and agreements carefully. Seek legal advice if necessary to ensure you understand the terms and obligations.

2. Model Rights: Familiarize yourself with your rights as a model, including the right to refuse assignments that make you uncomfortable or compromise your values.

3. Image Misuse: Be vigilant about image misuse. If you discover unauthorized use of your likeness, consult legal counsel about potential recourse.

4. Privacy: Respect your own privacy and the privacy of others. Avoid sharing personal information or images without consent.

As a professional model, your legal and ethical conduct is integral to your success and reputation in the industry. Always prioritize clear communication, respect for copyrights, and adherence to model release agreements when posting images on social media. By upholding high ethical standards and understanding your legal protections, you can navigate the modeling world with confidence and integrity.

16

LEGAL & ETHICAL CONSIDERATIONS

The modeling industry has undergone significant transformations in recent years, driven by technological advancements, changing consumer preferences, and a growing emphasis on diversity and inclusion. As a professional model, it's essential to stay ahead of these trends and prepare for the future. In this chapter, we'll explore the evolving landscape of modeling, including the rise of virtual castings, and provide insights on how to prepare for the industry's future.

THE EVOLUTION OF MODELING
1. Diversity and Inclusion: The industry has made strides in embracing diversity in terms of race, body type, gender, and age. There is a growing demand for models who represent a broader range of backgrounds and experiences.

2. Sustainability: Sustainable and ethical fashion is gaining momentum. Models who align with eco-friendly brands and practices are in high demand.

3. Virtual Castings: Virtual castings, powered by technology like augmented reality (AR) and virtual reality (VR), are changing how models are selected for assignments.

4. Social Media Influence: Social media influencers have a significant impact on the industry. Brands are collaborating with influencers to reach wider and more engaged audiences.

VIRTUAL CASTINGS: THE FUTURE OF MODEL SELECTION
Virtual castings, also known as digital castings, have become a prominent feature in the modeling industry. These castings rely on technology to evaluate models remotely, offering both opportunities and challenges:

1. Convenience: Virtual castings eliminate the need for physical attendance at auditions, making it more convenient for models and casting professionals.

2. Global Reach: Models can audition for international projects without leaving their location, expanding their opportunities.

3. Technology-Driven: Familiarize yourself with the

technology used in virtual castings, including video submissions, AR, and VR platforms.

4. Professionalism: Approach virtual castings with the same level of professionalism as in-person auditions. Ensure your video submissions are well-lit, high-quality, and showcase your versatility.

PREPARING FOR THE FUTURE
To succeed in the evolving modeling landscape, consider these strategies:

1. Digital Portfolio: Maintain an updated and comprehensive digital portfolio that showcases your versatility, diversity, and adaptability.

2. Tech Proficiency: Stay tech-savvy. Familiarize yourself with photo and video editing tools, as well as AR and VR platforms, to enhance your virtual presence.

3. Social Media Presence: Leverage social media to build your personal brand and connect with a global audience. Showcase your work, personality, and interests.

4. Diverse Skill Set: Diversify your skills. Explore acting, public speaking, and other talents that can enhance your modeling career.

5. Sustainability Awareness: Stay informed about sustainable fashion practices. Brands are increasingly seeking models who align with eco-conscious values.

6. Education: Continuously educate yourself about industry trends and emerging technologies. Attend workshops, webinars, and courses to stay updated.

7. Networking: Expand your network by connecting with professionals across the industry, including photographers, designers, agents, and casting directors.

8. Adaptability: Embrace change and remain adaptable. The modeling industry will continue to evolve, and flexibility is key to longevity.

The future of modeling is exciting and dynamic, marked by technological advancements, increased diversity, and new opportunities for global engagement. To thrive in this evolving landscape, models must remain adaptable, tech-savvy, and proactive in building their personal brand. Stay committed to your craft, remain open to change, and be prepared to embrace the limitless possibilities that the future of modeling offers.

17

YOUR MODELING JOURNEY BEGINS

Congratulations on embarking on your modeling journey and navigating the ins and outs of this dynamic and ever-evolving industry. Throughout this guide, we've explored every facet of the modeling profession, from developing your skills and building your portfolio to understanding the legal and ethical considerations that come with the territory. As you conclude this comprehensive journey, let's summarize key takeaways and outline your next steps.

KEY TAKEAWAYS
1. Preparation Is Key: Modeling success begins with preparation. Invest in your skills, portfolio, and personal brand to stand out in a competitive field.

2. Versatility Matters: Embrace versatility. The ability to adapt to various styles and projects can open doors to diverse opportunities.

YOUR MODELING JOURNEY BEGINS

3. Networking Is Essential: Building a strong network of industry professionals, mentors, and peers is crucial for growth and access to opportunities.

4. Ethical and Legal Awareness: Understand your rights and responsibilities as a model. Adhere to ethical standards and uphold professionalism.

5. Technology and Social Media: Stay tech-savvy and leverage social media to enhance your visibility and connect with your audience.

6. Sustainability and Inclusivity: Embrace sustainability and inclusivity trends in the industry. Align with brands that share your values.

7. Modeling in the Digital Age: Be prepared for virtual castings and the influence of technology in modeling. Adapt to emerging trends and technologies.

8. Future-Proofing Your Career: Continuously educate yourself, diversify your skills, and remain adaptable to thrive in the ever-evolving modeling landscape.

NEXT STEPS
As you conclude this guide, consider the following next steps on your modeling journey:

1. Continuous Growth: Commit to lifelong learning and skill development. Attend workshops, classes, and seminars to refine your craft.

2. Networking: Expand your network by attending industry events, collaborating with professionals, and seeking mentorship.

3. Diversify Your Portfolio: Keep your portfolio up to date with fresh, high-quality images that showcase your versatility.

4. Tech Mastery: Stay updated on technology trends in the industry. Familiarize yourself with virtual casting platforms and other emerging tools.

5. Stay Informed: Follow industry news and trends to remain informed about shifts in the fashion and modeling landscape.

6. Advocate for Diversity: Champion diversity and inclusivity within the industry. Be an advocate for change and fair representation.

7. Set Goals: Define your short-term and long-term goals. Create a roadmap for your career, complete with milestones and actionable steps.

8. Embrace Change: Embrace change with an open mind. Be ready to pivot and adapt to new opportunities and challenges.

Remember that your modeling journey is a unique and personal one. While this guide provides a comprehensive foundation, your path may take unexpected turns. Stay true to your vision, stay resilient, and maintain your passion for the art of modeling. Your dedication, professionalism, and creativity will carry you far in this exciting and rewarding profession.

Good luck on your journey!